THE PRICE OF MISSING LIFE

THE PRICE OF
MISSING LIFE

SIMON SCHROCK

ISBN: 0-89221-221-7
(previously ISBN: 0-8361-1980-0)

Library of Congress Catalog Number: 92-80704

Dedication

To my wife, Pauline, our children,
Janice Yvonne, Eldon Laverne, Ivan Dale,
and
the dedicated staff and co-workers
in the Choice Books ministry.

Contents

Author's Preface

A wise person will consider the cost of a project before plunging into it. If he doesn't, he may miss the mark and end in bankruptcy. Such a person may be considered a total failure.

Human beings have been created with physical bodies. Some things we do, food we eat, and habits we develop may be harmful to our bodies and devastating to our physical health. It is wise to count the cost of any chance we might take that would be a detriment to our physical well-being. The consequences of pain and suffering may not be worth the risk of short-lived pleasure. All too often we count only the cost of sacrifice for doing without. We forget to balance it out by counting the rewards or consequences that follow. It is wise to consider both.

As humans we have been created spiritual beings. To avoid spiritual failure, our spirit must come into a right relationship with our Creator. At the thought of coming into this right spiritual relationship with our Creator, we often heedlessly and recklessly count the cost of being believers and consider the cost as being too high-priced. We fail to take into account the cost of not believing.

Because of their failure to carefully consider the cost, many miss living faithful and meaningful lives. To miss life as God meant it to be lived carries an enormous price tag. In this book the reader is invited to compare and then count the cost of missing life as God planned it.

It is true, there is a price to pay for being a believer. It is also true that there is a high price to pay for not being a believer. It is my deep desire that individuals seriously count the cost of losing out and becoming spiritual failures. After counting the cost, the choice is of course up to each person. The choice is yours to make, but do consider the cost.

— Simon Schrock
Fairfax, Virginia

Introduction

The gospel is good news. It is the announcement of a personal God who opens himself to us in grace, accepts us in love, and involves himself in our experience. The acts of God in history, and His Word written, provide evidence which generates faith in our lives. Faith is the attitude which permits God to be himself in us. Participating in grace means sharing a transforming relationship with Christ.

In this book Simon Schrock presents in a simple and beautiful way the meaning of personal faith in Christ. Such faith is a deliberate choice as we respond to the Lord. The author calls the reader again and again to the awareness that Christian experience and fellowship with Christ save us from lostness here and now, and are worth the cost. It has been a joy to be reminded that Jesus became my Saviour in the experience of trust, and He is my Saviour in saving me today from being what I would have been without Him.

This book is a significant work in calling persons to personal faith in Christ. Christian faith is always personal but is never private.

Jesus calls us today to be His disciples, and in following Him we extend the meanings of faith into social practice through a living faith. I recommend this book to the reader as a pilgrimage in faith.

— Myron S. Augsburger
Washington, DC

1

Life Is for You

A young man once decided he wanted to become a Christian. However, after counting the cost he backed off and called it quits. The cost of a selfish ambition was too much for him.

There are many people who reason that they should become Christians, but the cost is too high. They aren't willing to give up their pleasures and ambitions for their lives. And they don't think they could live that kind of life. Although they covet the Christian's happiness and peace, the price is too high for them.

The young man who backed off was a rich young ruler who came to Jesus and asked what he had to do to inherit eternal life. After some discussion on the subject he walked off. The price was too high.

Life is for you. Jesus gives life. He said, "I am come that they might have life, and that they might have it more abundantly" (John 10:10). Jesus came to make a way for man to live life to the fullest. He came to give us all of life there is to be lived. That abundant life is for anyone.

One day a stranger named Jim Keens dropped by our Choice Books office. After a few minutes of conversation, I invited him to have a seat in my office. He told the account of how he received new life.

I was married at twenty-one and, because of the sinful life I was living, divorced at twenty-seven. The divorce tore my heart apart, but the only thing I could think of was myself.

Satan had blinded me to my sins. So I did not really think I was all that wrong or bad. Neither was I willing or able to face my sinfulness and deal with it. But then God began moving in on me.

At that time my daughter Dianne attended church regularly with a neighbor of my former wife. Sunday was my visitation day with Dianne, and one day during dinner together she said, "Daddy, God loves you." Tears filled my eyes, and I wondered what a five year old knew that I didn't.

Each Sunday I picked Dianne up after the church services. On the way to pick her up, I would stop at a People's Drug Store for a cup of coffee. One Sunday morning after finishing my cup of coffee, I noticed a book on a rack in the store. For some reason the book stood out to me and something inside me told me to buy it.

The book was entitled *World Aflame* and sounded exciting to read. I knew the author, Billy Graham, was a minister and I thought maybe I could find some answers to my messed-up life. So I bought the book.

The following Thursday was Thanksgiving Day, 1974. I was off from work and began reading the book. The more I read, the more clearly I saw I was on my way to hell. And it scared me. God used the message of this book to convict me of my sinfulness.

I came to a page in that book that had a prayer to pray if you wanted Jesus to come into your life and forgive your sins. I knew if I was really sincere in my heart, Jesus would save me.

I laid the book face up on the couch, got down on my knees, and asked God to forgive me of my sins. I told Him that I was sorry for my sins and wanted Jesus to come into my heart and save me.

God, of course, was true to His Word. That very moment He saved me and changed my life. I drove immediately to the home of a Christian couple and told them what I had done and asked them to pray for me.

The following Sunday I accompanied my daughter to church and went forward to make a public confession of my faith in Christ and God.

My life is now lived for Jesus Christ, who died for my sins at Calvary. The Holy Spirit has given me a tremendous desire for God's Word and has enabled me to lead several people to Jesus. I praise God for His only begotten Son, Jesus, and His willingness to die for my sins.

Jim came to Jesus and received life. He was born again by the Spirit of God. He now enjoys life and lives with a purpose.

Having life means we live life to the fullest. And that takes place here and now while we are on Earth. It also means we have the hope of heaven after we take our last breath. Being a Christian means we have life here and hereafter.

Yes, it does cost to be a Christian disciple in today's world. The price is high.

On the other hand, what is the cost of not being a Christian? Isn't that also high-priced? To be a non-Christian has at least a dozen expensive price tags attached. The unbeliever pays those price tags. Let's examine the first price tag of not believing.

To choose not to believe, to not become a Christian, costs us abundant life. Jesus said, "He that believeth not is condemned already" (John 3:18). Jesus told of a rich man who missed life. This rich man "dressed in the most expensive clothes and lived in great luxury every day" (Luke 16:19; TEV). From a worldly standard he had it made. But he missed life.

This rich man died and was buried. "And in hell he lift up his eyes, being in torments, and seeth Abraham afar off, and Lazarus in his bosom. And he cried and said, Father Abraham, have mercy on me, and send Lazarus, that he may dip the tip of his finger in water, and cool my tongue; for I am tormented in this flame" (Luke 16:23,24).

Here was a man who had had everything on this Earth. Now he was begging for one drop of life. Jesus said, "I am the bread of life: he that cometh to me shall never hunger; and he that believeth on me shall never thirst" (John 6:35). This rich man missed the thirst-quenching life. He will be eternally paying the price for missing life and taking his own selfish way.

Imagine yourself on a hot summer day with

the temperature nearly 100 degrees. You're work-ing in the hot sun, digging a ditch for your employer. Soaked wet with sweat and nearly exhausted, you are in dire need of a drink. You look up and see a pitcher of iced lemonade through the picture window. However, there is a window and a locked door between you and the lemonade and you can't get it. You are thirsty, but can't reach the lemonade. The rich man was thirsty for life, but it was now out of reach.

One price tag for not being a Christian is the cost of missing life. It is missing life abundant here and now, and life eternal hereafter. It is a high price to pay for missing something so good.

2

You Can Be Free

How do your bad deeds compare to your good deeds on a balancing scale? A popular notion exists that if a person has done more good deeds than bad, he will be accepted into heaven when he dies. Another idea is that even though a person is 49 percent bad, if he is 51 percent good, he is on safe ground. That is, if the evil and the good in a person are balanced against each other, and the good outweighs the bad, that will gain favor with God.

There are several problems with such ideas. First, we can never be quite sure when we have done more good than bad. At what point do the scales tip to 51 percent positive? What great deeds will balance the evil with good? It is especially difficult to be sure when we reflect on the lack of progress accomplished in reaching our goal.

Just when a person may feel good about himself, he may let his anger burst into violence. In his anger he may attack the character of a loved one. These actions move the scales into the negative.

The second problem with trying to balance scales is that good deeds done will not correct wrongs committed in the past. They will not change the heart which is the source of all actions. Nor will they bring justice for past wrong deeds.

The third problem is that trying to outweigh bad deeds with good simply doesn't work. The Bible tells us that "all have sinned, and come short of the glory of God" (Rom. 3:23). At another point it says, "There is none righteous, no, not one" (Rom. 3:10). The prophet Isaiah described it this way: "All we like sheep have gone astray; we have turned every one to his own way" (Isa. 53:6). Another prophet, Jeremiah, said, "The heart is deceitful above all things, and desperately wicked" (Jer. 17:9).

When the first man, Adam, disobeyed God, he brought sin into the human race. This sin contaminated his nature. Adam's sin nature was passed on to his children and his children's children. It was passed on to all people. Therefore, all people are born with the sin nature of selfishness. The apostle Paul confirmed this when he said, "all have sinned."

This sin nature that was introduced into the world by Adam's choice must be dealt with by each individual. Justice must be done. Balancing the scales with good deeds will not take away the sinful nature nor will it satisfy justice. It will not bring righteousness in the sight of a just and Holy God. Neither will it change man's deceitful heart which Jeremiah wrote about. Man is always found "short of the glory of God" on the balancing scales. The balancing out of the scales can never totally satisfy man's deep inner desire to make peace with a Holy God.

More than 100 years ago President Lincoln signed the Emancipation Proclamation. The signing meant that persons held as slaves were to be set free. This proclamation included orders for the law enforcement authorities to recognize and maintain freedom for the slaves. The president's signature permitted slaves to leave bondage if they chose to do so.

Mankind is a slave. We are slaves to Adam's sin nature. His sinful nature has been passed on to all people and now everyone is enslaved to sin. As mentioned before, the Bible says that "all have sinned" and that "there is none righteous, no, not one." It comes down to the fact that all of us have a sinful nature, and have sinned. Therefore we are all slaves and servants to sin.

However, One came to sign our proclamation of emancipation. That person is Jesus Christ. He came to seek and save those who are slaves to sin and lost in its grip of bondage.

Jesus Christ came into the world to take upon himself the penalty that justice demands for Adam's sin. He came to take the penalty of every person's sin, which is what Christ did on the cross. When He went to that cross He took upon himself the punishment for sin. He loved mankind so much that He painfully took our punishment on that cross.

The price of sin was paid when He shed His blood and then cried out, "It is finished." In that statement He meant that He had done all that could be done on his part to set us free. "It is finished" is humanity's proclamation of emancipation.

Christ is the emancipation *if* mankind accepts Him. The good news is that Jesus gives forgiveness and acceptance. Sinful persons who came to Him for pardon received it. To the woman taken in the very act of adultery, He said, "Neither do I condemn thee: go, and sin no more" (John 8:11). To the thief on the cross who asked for mercy, Jesus said, "Today shalt thou be with me in paradise" (Luke 23:43).

Another example is the sinful woman who intruded upon the dinner that Simon the Pharisee put on for Jesus. While they were dining, the woman came in and began weeping, then washed the feet of Jesus with her tears of sorrow. This same woman had the nerve to use her hair to wipe His feet. Jesus told her, "Thy sins are forgiven . . . Thy faith hath saved thee; go in peace" (Luke 7:48,50).

Christians are people who have taken their sin case to Jesus. They are the people who have accepted Christ's invitation to believe on Him and receive forgiveness. The Bible tells us, "If we confess our sins, he is faithful and just to forgive us our sins, and to cleanse us from all unrighteousness" (1 John 1:9). To become a Christian means you must confess your sinfulness to Christ, and ask forgiveness. Christ takes the sin case to the Heavenly Father. Forgiveness is promised through Christ who paid the penalty for sin on the cross. When we sincerely ask for forgiveness, we will receive it. It is God's gift to set us free from sin's penalty.

An effective business keeps a file cabinet. Whenever a transaction is made, a record is filed. Debts, purchases, and payments due are kept on record. Sometimes debts pile up and become too much to pay. The records on file show then that the liabilities exceed the assets in such a way that it is impossible for the business to meet the obligations or recover the former financial standing. The business is broke, bankrupt, a total failure.

That is how we stand in God's file cabinet. Our sinfulness and sins are so great there is no way to meet the obligations. Without God we are broke; we are bankrupt and total failures. This is the reason God sent His Son, Jesus, to shed His blood in full payment of our debt. Therefore when we come to God believing and asking for His forgiveness, the blood Christ shed removes the sin debt accumulated in the files. His blood makes the record clean. Being Christians gives us the satisfaction of knowing that God has cleared all debts and set us free. We Christians can rest our case with the heavenly Father.

The late J.C. Brumfield wrote about a train traveling through a violent storm during the night. The passengers were seized with terror. In the midst of it all one little girl was perfectly peaceful. Someone asked her how she could possibly be so calm when the rest were so worried. She smiled sweetly and said, "My father is the engineer." The Christian can rest his case with the heavenly Father and be assured that he is in the hands of a good engineer.

John wrote a message of forgiveness in the Bible. To that message He added these words: "These things have I written unto you that believe on the name of the Son of God; that ye may know that ye have eternal life, and that ye may believe on the name of the Son of God" (1 John 5:13).

Being a Christian means we have accepted God's forgiveness and assurance. God has made a promise and He has been taken at His word. The sin debt is canceled and we can go free from the penalty of condemnation. That is good news for rejoicing.

On the other hand, if we choose not to become a Christian and not to believe, the sin debt is not canceled. We are still accountable and liable, never sure if we are on solid ground or if we are good enough. We have to live unforgiven, in doubt and distress. That is not good news. To not become a Christian costs us forgiveness and assurance.

Is it worth it?

3

Go in Peace

Our world has many fearful people. People fear one another. They fear crime, violence, theft, and loss of property. They fear economic calamity. Some fear to walk around the corner to the drugstore. Many fear themselves. People fear failure, even life and death, and the future looks dark and fearful to them.

People today are much like the man Jesus referred to who was given one talent to use. This man said, "I was afraid, and went and hid thy talent in the earth" (Matt. 25:25). They are afraid to use their talents in becoming who and what God wants them to be.

When I was a little boy, I had to cross the creek in back of our barn to bring the cows in from the back field. There was a large foot log across the creek that was used for a crosswalk. Crossing that log was a scary task for me. I remember one day I was part way out on the log when I looked down and saw how far it was to the water and became frightened. It was a case where I was afraid to go on and afraid to go back. It is at that point where many people find themselves in life, fearing the future and the past.

Jesus came to such a fearful world to bring peace. He came to bring peace on Earth into the hearts and lives of those who would come to Him.

Jesus was invited to lunch one day by Simon, a Pharisee. Jesus accepted the invitation and went to dine at Simon's house. While they were at lunch, a prostitute learned He was there. This wicked woman intruded upon the lunch engagement to be with Jesus and have Him fill her need. The need was peace.

She came to Jesus crying for help, and her tears of regret and sorrow dripped on His feet. This prostitute then dried His feet with the hair of her head and tenderly kissed Jesus' feet. Then she anointed His feet with a costly perfume.

When this fearful woman with many sins brought her case to the Son of God, He told her, "Thy sins are forgiven thee." Then He said to the woman, "Thy faith hath saved thee; go in peace" (Luke 7:50).

Go in peace. Those are the words of Jesus, and that is what He is offering people who come to Him. Coming to Jesus means becoming a Christian. Becoming a Christian means we can go in peace because we have taken our case to Jesus and rested it with Him.

This is a world of rush and confusion. The jet age is polluting our skies with fumes and noises, and while we breathe airplane smoke, we are wheezing for air. Poison has been absorbed into our food; we have diseases we can't conquer. Affluent living has left us wanting, and we are under the threat of a push-button blowup. Technology has given us more trouble than we can get out of.

And so modern man, after the late show, after his Pepsi, after Miller time, rolls and turns on his restless bed and thinks there must be more to life.

Many people wonder if there isn't more to life than what the world offers. They are right — there is more. To a world like this Jesus came to bring peace on Earth. He came to tell people, "Go in peace."

Picture a factory bellowing its grimy smoke into the air. Hear the noisy assembly line. The clattering freight trains. The roaring jet overhead. The honking horns and deafening engines of cars, trucks, and motorcycles roaring across the asphalt jungles of parking lots and highways.

Then picture a lonely tree in the midst of a hot parking lot. There in the tree a robin is singing bird-praises while his mate sits calmly on the eggs in her nest. Above the noise and rush of a dirty factory, those birds are at peace in the midst of confusion.

We Christians can be like the robins. We live in a world of confusion, but we are at peace. Our inner peace is not totally determined by what surrounds us. We are at peace in spite of our environment. This peace is because of our relationship with the Christ who came through closed doors and stood in the midst of His disciples and said, "Peace be unto you" (Luke 24:36). He has committed his life to the One who showed His disciples the nail scars in His hands and feet and then said, "Peace be unto you."

Peace does not come from where we are or what we own, but by whom we know. To know Jesus is to know peace.

Christians can be at peace because we have committed our life to the One whose word even the wind and sea obey. One day when Jesus was teaching the people with many parables, He asked His disciples to go to the other side of the sea. While they were sailing, the tired Teacher fell asleep. En route there arose a great wind and storm that blew water into the ship and almost caused it to sink. The frightened disciples awakened Jesus and asked if He didn't care that they were perishing.

Jesus arose and rebuked the wind and said to the sea, "Peace, be still" (Mark 4:39). The wind ceased and there was a perfect calmness. Just as Jesus calmed the sea, so He came to bring calm and peace to your life.

Jesus himself said, "Peace I leave with you, my peace I give unto you; not as the world giveth, give I unto you. Let not your heart be troubled, neither let it be afraid" (John 14:27).

The prophet Isaiah said, "Thou wilt keep him in perfect peace, whose mind is stayed on thee" (Isa. 26:3).

Peter invited the Christian to place all his cares, problems, and burdens on God in 1 Peter 5:7, "Casting all your care upon him; for he careth for you." The Christian is asked to cast all his concerns and anxieties upon God. Being a Christian means knowing a God who cares. Knowing a God who cares gives one peace.

An elderly Christian brother related to me some of the meditations he had during a recent hospital experience. While he was gravely ill he thought of the many sins of his past. Although he had confessed them a time back, he still regretted them. He had problems forgiving himself. Then he thought of Christ and His love, and he felt someone saying to him, "Let me have your problems." He released them and then he was at peace.

Jesus came to take our problems so we can be at peace. The Bible says, "Therefore being justified by faith, we have peace with God through our Lord Jesus Christ" (Rom. 5:1). Placing our faith and trust in Jesus Christ gives us peace with God. Having peace with God, yourself, and others is what being a Christian is all about.

In this world of confusion, peace is a prized treasure. It belongs uniquely to the person who trusts and knows Jesus Christ as Saviour and Lord.

On the other hand we forfeit peace if we choose not to be Christians. To not know the "Prince of Peace" means to be a part of the world of confusion, to be in this world without peace, without peace for eternity.

Jesus gives peace. To miss Him means missing peace.

Is it worth it?

4

Joyful Living

It was a hot and humid Virginia July. We were preparing to set up a book display at a gathering called Fishnet, near Front Royal, Virginia. This was an important event on our calendar. Thousands of people would be gathered for the weekend, and Choice Books would have the book display and provide books for sale. During this busy time came the call that my father was gravely ill.

I telephoned my family frequently from the scene of the meeting. Each time I phoned the report was less hopeful. My wife and I decided to leave that night to be with my family through the experience. We drove the winding roads of West Virginia to my mountain home.

We arrived during the night and upon entering the house we learned that Dad was no longer there. He had been taken to the hospital in Morgantown, West Virginia, and he was rapidly slipping into a coma.

Tests showed that Dad had a blood clot on the brain. The doctors explained to our family that surgery was an option. At the age of eighty, with a strong heart and a body that hadn't used alcohol or tobacco, they gave him about a fifty-fifty chance. The possibility of his speech returning was less hopeful.

Dad was taken to surgery. The operation was performed and he survived. He began to recover remarkably well. Ten days later my father was released from the hospital.

My older brother and I helped him from the hospital wheelchair into the carefully prepared bed in the back of my station wagon. We cautiously drove the steep winding mountainous roads toward home. The scenery of green fields and mountain slopes was beautiful! The thought that we were actually bringing my father home alive overtook us with joy. At times tears flooded our eyes. Dad was alive! We were overwhelmed with joy.

Nearly 2,000 years ago Jesus Christ was nailed to a cross. He was crucified and left hanging on the cross to die. His death was a stunning blow to His friends and followers. They were crushed with sadness and grief at the realization that the soldiers had killed their master. The cold reality was that Jesus had died.

Joseph, one of Jesus' followers, begged to have the body of Jesus for burial. Pilate granted his request. Joseph took the body of Jesus, wrapped it in a clean linen cloth, and buried it in a tomb which had been prepared for himself when he died. A great stone was rolled in front of the door of the grave. Pilate commanded that the tomb be sealed and guarded so no one would steal the body of Jesus and claim He rose from the dead.

After the Sabbath, as Sunday morning was dawning, two women, Mary and Mary Magdalene, went to see the tomb. There was a great earthquake and the angel of the Lord came from heaven to roll away the sealed stone and sit on it. His appearance was like lightning and his clothes were white as snow. The guards were so afraid they trembled and shook and looked like dead men.

Then the angel spoke to the women and told them not to be afraid. The angel recognized they were looking for the body of Jesus who had been crucified. He assured them, saying, "He is not here; for He is risen, as He said" (Matt. 28:6). The angel then charged the women to go tell Jesus' disciples that He was risen from the dead and that they would see Him in Galilee.

Imagine, the dead Christ alive! Today people

say to each other, "See you at work" or "See you tomorrow." The angel assured the women that Jesus would see them in Galilee. With such astounding news they left in a hurry to tell their friends.

They hurried away fearfully, yet filled with great joy. The great joy came because Jesus was alive! My brother and I were filled with joy that day we were able to bring my father home alive from the hospital. These two women were filled with great joy because He who died had risen and was alive. Truly that was great joy!

Jesus is more alive now than ever. Death has no grip on Him. He came to the edge of the valley of the shadow of death and He went on through with it. He personally experienced death and tasted it for all mankind. He conquered it. He arose more alive than ever. He is now untouchable by death. Because He lives, we too can live.

Mary and Mary Magdalene experienced great joy when they found themselves in the presence of the living Christ. Being a Christian means we too partake of this great joy. Joy becomes ours when we believe because Christ is a living Savior. Joy is ours because He offers forgiveness and pardon to those who seek it. There is joy because He is preparing a mansion for the believers and there is joy because He will come again and receive the Christians unto himself. As Jesus said, "Where I am, there ye may be also" (John 14:3).

The Christian has great joy because the same Spirit that raised Jesus from the dead now lives in the believer's life. What does this mean? It means that the same Spirit that gave life to Jesus then gives life to the believer now. The Spirit that brought Jesus out of the tomb brings the believer out of sin and darkness into light and life. Where there were despair and death, the Spirit gives great joy, hope, and life to those who come to Jesus. It is no wonder that the Bible tells us that "the disciples were filled with joy" (Acts 13:52).

The new life Jesus promised is here now. Jesus is alive and His Spirit lives in the believer. His Spirit changes people from old guilty persons into new free persons. When Jesus makes new persons, old things pass away and everything becomes new. Christ is changing people from drunkenness to fulfilled living. He makes men of love from angry men and makes mean individuals into kind characters. He changes thieves into persons giving of themselves for the good of others.

The Spirit of the living Christ is bringing people into new love relationships. Husbands and wives who turn to Him are experiencing new love and understanding. Families are changing from chaotic existences into loving relationships of forgiveness, understanding, and respect for one another. All of this means great joy deep within the hearts of the people who experience His love.

The apostle Paul explained it like this: "the kingdom of God is not meat and drink; but righteousness, and peace, and joy in the Holy Ghost" (Rom. 14:17).

Peter explains the result of believing as "joy unspeakable and full of glory" (1 Pet. 1:8).

John writes an epistle and says, "These things write we unto you, that your joy may be full" (1 John 1:4).

What does John write of interest about our joy? He testifies of seeing and hearing Jesus. He proclaims that God is light, and if we walk in that light we have fellowship with another. He further declares that if we walk in the light, the blood of Jesus Christ, God's Son, cleans us from all sin.

Then comes more good news! If we confess our sins, God will forgive us and cleanse us of them. Why does John write these good things? Because joy is for us. He wants us to partake of the joy Jesus offers. "These things write we unto you, that your joy may be full."

Jesus told His audience, "These things have I spoken unto you, that my joy might remain in you, and that your joy may be full" (John 15:11). The joyful message He spoke contained words of life. He explained that if we abide in Him, He abides in us. He said He is the vine and Christians are the branches. Jesus is the vine, the very center of life. If we are attached to Him we are attached to life and being attached to life will make us fruitful. Our life will produce fruit and that means we will fulfill an important role in life. In Christ each of us is somebody.

Jesus is interested in seeing lives produce much fruit. He said, "If ye abide in me, and my words abide in you, ye shall ask what ye will, and it shall be done unto you" (John 15:7). This is a fruit-producing promise. When we abide in Him, He makes us productive people in His kingdom.

Jesus spoke these joy words so we may be joyous and so that our joy cup will be full. He wants us to participate totally in life with Him. He wants us to partake and share in His joy. Christians have a deep inward joy that the world can't take away.

It is no wonder that the disciples were filled with this same joy. Christ gave them a purpose to fulfill and a mission to accomplish. In Christ they became persons of high value in God's plan for the future. God needs and calls persons to carry on His plan that began at creation and reaches into the new world that is coming. When one is abiding in Christ, he becomes that kind of person. He belongs to an important work. That produces joy.

There was an important Ethiopian official who was in charge of the treasury. He was on his way home from Jerusalem. As he rode along in his carriage he read from the book of the prophet Isaiah. However he didn't understand what he was reading.

Philip, one of Christ's followers, was sent by an angel of the Lord to explain to this official what the word of Isaiah meant. Philip explained to him the good news about Jesus that he was reading. The official then wanted to be baptized. Philip said he could be baptized if he believed in Jesus with all his heart. The official answered, "I believe that Jesus Christ is the Son of God" (Acts 8:37). The carriage was stopped, they went to the water, and Philip baptized the Ethiopian. The official went on his way rejoicing.

That is what happens when a person places his faith and trust in Jesus. He goes on his way rejoicing. He can be joyous because now there is hope for the present and for the future.

Today people around the world are experiencing the joy of life in Jesus. This joy crosses over cultural and racial barriers to all believers.

Webster's dictionary defines joy as gladness, happiness, a deep spiritual experience. That is what the Christian possesses. He has a deep inner joy that cannot be replaced with anything the world offers.

On the other hand, the high cost of not being a Christian is not having joy now and forever.

Is it worth it?

5

Know Where You're Going

It's a fascinating scene to stand near the edge of the Washington National Airport runway and watch the constant flow of airplanes taking off and landing. As pilots receive directions from the control tower, they land the big jets on the runways. Each day the control tower directs hundreds of pilots to safely land the jetliners. Because the pilots receive and follow directions, thousands of people are safely transported in and out of the airport. Losing contact with the control tower may mean disaster.

In the spring of 1977, on the Canary Islands,

two 747 jumbo jets crashed during takeoff. When one pilot lost his sense of direction, his jet crashed into the other one. It was suggested that takeoff had not been granted, and the instructions from the control tower, in plain English, were ignored. It was a disaster. Five hundred and eighty-two people died in the worst crash in civil aviation history. Was it because directions were ignored?

Jesus gives directions to His followers. A believer knows the direction he is going. Jesus, His Word, and His Spirit are the Christian's spiritual radar control tower. Christians enjoy the blessings of receiving directions for living. Wise Solomon said of God's guidance, "Trust in the Lord with all thine heart; and lean not unto thine own understanding. In all thy ways acknowledge him, and he shall direct thy paths" (Prov. 3:5,6). The believer who trusts and acknowledges God is assured of God's guidance. He will direct the Christian's ways.

The prophet Isaiah said, "The Lord God shall guide thee continually" (Isa. 58:11). David wrote in Psalm 32:8, "I will instruct thee and teach thee in the way which thou shalt go."

Godly men in the past have experienced God's guidance. Abraham was guided to a land that God told him would be "unto thy seed." In another incident God told Abraham to take his only son, Isaac, to the land of Moriah and sacrifice him for a burnt offering. God told Abraham the specific mountain to which he was to go. Abraham followed God in detail to the place where he was instructed. There he built an altar, placed the wood in order, and tied his son for the sacrifice to God. As he was ready to bring down the knife to slay Isaac, the angel of the Lord called out of heaven and said, "Lay not thine hand upon the lad, neither do thou any thing unto him: for now I know that thou fearest God, seeing thou hast not withheld thy son, thine only son from me" (Gen. 22:12).

When Abraham looked up, he saw a beast that was caught in the thick bushes by his horns. Abraham offered the animal for a sacrifice instead of his son Isaac. God tested His servant Abraham in this experience, and at the same time guided him to a place where there was a ram caught, ready for sacrifice.

Moses and the children of Israel experienced guidance over and over again as they left Egypt. In the daytime God went before them in a pillar of cloud, and at night in a pillar of fire. God gave Moses the Ten Commandments of guidance for their well-being.

Hezekiah experienced guidance when God sent an angel to cut off the mighty men of the enemy camp and led the king and the inhabitants of Jerusalem to safety. The Bible says the Lord "guided them on every side" (2 Chron. 32:22).

God's guidance was again demonstrated

when He sent a bright star to guide and lead the wise men directly to the place where Jesus was. God gives His people directions.

Jesus said, "I am the door: by me if any man enter in, he shall be saved, and shall go in and out, and find pasture" (John 10:9). Jesus is the door to a guided way. To go through the Jesus door is to enter into fellowship with Him and to walk with Someone who knows the way. In fact, Jesus said, "I am the way" (John 14:6). Since Jesus himself is the way, He will be the One to guide us along the way.

Directions for living! How does God give them to His followers? First, He gives them through His Word, which is recorded in the Bible. This book is often referred to as the road map to heaven. It is God's guidance manual for mankind. Another way God guides is by His Holy Spirit. God's Holy Spirit is a gift to the believers that guides them into truth.

God also gives guidance and direction through fellowship in the Christian Church. As a believer studies God's Word with God's people, he learns more about God's will for his life. He may seek counsel from fellow believers in specific situations. God often gives directions through other Christians who understand the problem and what God's Word says about it.

The Bible gives direction. It is God's guidebook to man. The Psalmist said of God's Word, "Thy word is a lamp unto my feet, and a light unto my path" (Ps. 119:105). The Bible itself tells us that "all scripture is given by inspiration of God, and is profitable for doctrine, for reproof, for correction, for instruction in righteousness: that the man of God may be perfect, thoroughly furnished unto all good works" (2 Tim. 3:16,17).

This passage states that the guidebook has been inspired by God. It is God-breathed. He directed the writers to write His message. It also says that it is profitable for "instruction in righteousness." God's Word is a valuable book by which we receive guidance for living.

I had the privilege to ride to the top of Mt. Evans in Colorado. This Rocky Mountain peak is 14,264 feet high, the highest point in the United States that can be reached by automobile. From the top it was a beautiful sight to behold the panoramic view of the landscape. Many miles down at the bottom there is a lake which was visible from various points on the drive up the mountain. Before we started our climb up the narrow, winding road I noticed some people fishing from this lake.

This illustrates what the Bible can mean to the believer. He can get a mountain top view of the book by reading the entire contents. That will give him an idea of God's total plan for history. Then he can go fishing. As he digs into chapters, verses, parables, and even word meanings, he catches new truths that will help him to better understand the guidebook. The Word tells us to "study to shew thyself approved unto God" (2 Tim. 2:15). The Bible is a book of guidance for the Christian.

Another guide God gives the believer is the gift of God's Holy Spirit dwelling within him. Jesus said, "I will pray the Father, and he shall give you another Comforter, that he may abide with you for ever" (John 14:16). Jesus said of the Spirit, "He shall teach you all things" (John 14:26).

The believer who invites Jesus into his life to be Lord and ruler has the Spirit residing in himself. The Holy Spirit takes up residence in that person's life. The Scripture says, "Know ye not that your body is the temple of the Holy Ghost?" (1 Cor. 6:19). The Good News Bible says it this way: "Don't you know that your body is the temple of the Holy Spirit, who lives in you and who was given to you by God?"

To believe in and to yield to the lordship of Jesus means having the guiding Holy Spirit actually living and residing within us. Jesus said this residing Spirit "will guide you into all truth" (John 16:13).

The Christian who asks the Spirit to preside in his life also experiences receiving directions from Him in the fullest measure. The one who yields his right-of-way to the Holy Spirit and invites Him to become president, director, and ruler of his life discovers a power to live Godly and differently in this world.

When the Spirit occupies the principal place in the believer's life, he experiences a fellowship with God that goes beyond a set of rules to live by. His life conduct is more than a code of ethics. It becomes a life of joyful, willful, and loving obedience as he walks with the living Lord whose Spirit calls the directions.

It reminds me of a backhoe in the hands of a good operator. The operator sits on the seat pushing and pulling levers. As the big scoop receives directions it digs, picks up the dirt, lifts it high, and dumps it into a truck. It continues at the command of the operator until the job is completed.

A person who invites the Holy Spirit to occupy the operator's seat of his life yields himself as controls to the hands of the Holy Spirit. The Spirit directs his life into useful channels that accomplish a job well. As believers, we can experience the abiding presence and the direction from God through the Spirit that dwells within us.

The third place the believer receives directions from God is through Christian fellowship, the Church. Christ's Church is a body of believers who work together for the good and well-being of one another. They are a group of people who are concerned for one another and share in each other's joys and sorrows. They feel the hurts and needs of each other.

Together they seek directions from God on

how to live fulfilling lives. They can tackle problems, concerns, and frustrations because they are a family of God. Being a part of a caring church helps them in receiving direction.

A caring church can come together and seek God's wisdom for problems they are facing. The Bible tells them to ask God for wisdom: "If any of you lack wisdom, let him ask of God" (James 1:5). When a person asks God for wisdom he can expect God's response. The *Good News Bible* says, "He should pray to God, who will give it to him; because God gives generously and graciously to all" (James 1:5).

God wants us to ask and He wants to give. A caring church can pull together the insights and wisdom of a broad base of varied experiences. The church can consider together the thinking and discerning of all ages from teens to grandfathers. Someone in the fellowship may have been over the problem area before and therefore could testify of its dangers. Others may have a better alternative to offer.

A believer may share his problems with individuals within the church body. Often he will be able to discern what direction to take as he shares his frustrations and doubts with others who deeply care for him as a person.

I recall an incident where several of us young brethren in the church had a big idea for evangelism. As we shared the idea with another brother in the church, we discovered problems he saw that we hadn't seen from our perspective. He suggested an alternative idea.

As I look back I see the wisdom of his advice and I've never been sorry that we accepted his suggestion. It was a much better course of action and we didn't wreck our reputation by following it.

Directions for a believer can come from a believing fellowship. To not be a part of such a fellowship costs you the counsel of other mature believers whose vast experience could be a rich asset to your life.

As you stand near Washington's airport you can observe the big jets making their touchdown on the runway. The control tower beams out directions for a safe landing. The passengers can leave the plane and go on to fulfill their duties.

God's children operate on the directions from His control tower. He leads them into purposeful living. When they are directed by God, their lives are used as a contribution to mankind. God used Moses to direct and manage a people He had chosen for himself. Moses' life was used in many notable events of history. He is listed with the men of faith. Moses took directions from God.

To be Christians means we are not living aimlessly or without a purpose. Instead, we are steered on course by God's radar — the Bible, the Holy Spirit, and His Church.

Each cost of not believing is expensive. Choosing not to believe costs us the very way to life — Jesus. It also costs us the guidance of God's Word, the abiding of the Holy Spirit, and the benefits of a caring fellowship.

Is it worth it?

6

A New You

Suppose I could push a button right now that would leave you unable to ever change. If you are not a Christian, you would have to remain that way. If you raise your voice at your wife when things don't go your way, you would always raise your voice. If you pout in silence when you get upset, you would always have to contend with your own pouting. If you are critical of others, you would remain an unpleasant critic.

Do you want to always remain the same person you are now? Are you satisfied with your ability to love others and express kindness to those around you? Or do you sometimes feel that you aren't the person you should be?

The Bible records accounts of two men who kept company with Jesus who were less than their best in behavior. One of these men was Judas Iscariot. He schemed to sell the Lord to his oppressors for thirty pieces of silver. In his book, *Let's Face It*, Bruce Shelly says Judas "sold Jesus for the price of a common slave. Judas certainly demonstrated that this was not the best in behavior and conduct." He was a selfish, unkind, and unloving person.

That same selfish and unkind nature is in all of us. However, the important questions are: Do I always want to be the same unkind, selfish me? Will I have to remain this way with no chance of change? Judas never changed. He went out and hanged himself. The Bible gives this description of his gruesome ending: "This man purchased a field with the reward of iniquity; and falling headlong, he burst asunder in the midst, and all his bowels gushed out" (Acts 1:18). Judas ended all possibility of becoming a new person.

The other one of Jesus' associates was Peter who left his fishing to follow Jesus. He saw Jesus heal his mother-in-law. He saw Him heal Jairus' daughter. He was present at the transfiguration experience. At Christ's invitation Peter walked on water. And yet, after all of this, Peter was caught in the act of revenge and outright lying. He was caught at his worst and he was less than the person he really wanted to be.

When the soldiers came to capture Jesus, Peter was ready to fight. He took a sword and slashed off an ear of the servant of the high priest. Following this incident, Peter lied three times. He was sitting outside the courtyard where Jesus was being tried. One of the high priest's servant girls recognized that he was one of those with Jesus of Galilee. When he was questioned he denied it. In the presence of the servant of the high priest he claimed he didn't know what she was talking about.

Later, another servant saw him and said, "This fellow was also with Jesus of Nazareth" (Matt. 26:71). This time Peter not only lied, but he used an oath with the lie. A little later, the men standing around Peter told him that by his speech they could tell he was one of those who were with Jesus. This time Peter cursed, swore and lied, saying he didn't know the man.

Then a rooster crowed and Peter recalled the words of Jesus, when He told Peter he would deny Him three times before a rooster crowed. The sound of that rooster sent a shock through Peter and reminded him that he was not at his best. He had lied. He had cursed and sworn. His behavior had hit bottom. Did he stay the same old liar, the same bottomed-out bum? No! He changed.

It is in this man Peter that the Scripture truth in 2 Corinthians 5:17 is truly demonstrated. It says, "Therefore if any man be in Christ, he is a new creature: old things are passed away; behold, all things are become new."

So to be a Christian we need not always be the same person. We need not always be an unkind, selfish, arrogant character. God's Spirit power can change us. That is what Peter experienced when God's Spirit took up residence in his spirit and changed his life. This man who lied about his identification with Christ didn't remain a liar. He returned to Christ and became a new person whose ministry is still blessing people today.

The new Peter was used by the Spirit of God to preach God's Word in a powerful way. He was used to heal the sick. He was the instrument God used to raise Dorcas from the dead. He advocated the preaching of the good news to the gentiles. An angel of the Lord delivered him from prison. He wrote two epistles of the Bible. The "newborn" Peter was a changed person. The life and teaching of the new Peter have helped people around the world find new life. Peter definitely became a new person in Christ.

Therefore, when one believes, he becomes a new person. He can grow into the likeness of Christ as he walks with Him day by day. To believe is to become a new you.

To believe means we trade our unrighteousness and sinfulness for the gift of God's righteousness. The Bible says it like this: "For he hath made him to be sin for us, who knew no sin; that we might be made the righteousness of God in him" (2 Cor. 5:21).

This means that Jesus went before God the Father and pleaded our cause as He handled our case of sinfulness. He became the sin offering for us. Whatever the charge was against us, Jesus had it placed on His account. Our sinfulness is taken from our balance due and placed upon Christ's account which is already paid in full. In exchange Christ's righteousness is placed on our account as we trade sin for righteousness.

The apostle Paul wrote to his friend Philemon on behalf of another person named Onesimus. Onesimus was headed in the wrong direction and was an unprofitable servant. He was a boy who had left and become bad. However, he did change and he returned. Paul wrote to Philemon and asked him to receive Onesimus as a partner, just as he would receive Paul himself. He further wrote that if Onesimus wronged Philemon or if he owed him anything, Philemon should put it on Paul's account.

That is what Jesus did to make each one of us a new person. He hung on the cross between heaven and earth, paying up our account. He hung there in the presence of His scoffers and those who crucified Him, paying our sin debt. He hung dying before God the Father with the attitude that whatever the charge had been, it should be put to His account.

All the penalty we owed was charged to Jesus. He hung between the gap of our sinfulness and God's perfect righteousness. He paid the debt that was on our account and cleared everything that was charged against us. He did this so that we could become right before God and then become a new person.

How do we get our account cleared and have it transferred to Christ's account? Jesus told a parable of two men who went into the temple to pray. One was a Pharisee and the other a publican, a tax collector. The Pharisee stood praying and said to himself, "God, I thank thee, that I am not as other men are, extortioners, unjust, adulterers, or even as this publican. I fast twice in the week, I give tithes of all that I possess" (Luke 18:11).

The tax collector was standing at a distance and wouldn't as much as lift his eyes toward heaven, but beat upon his breast and said, "God be merciful to me a sinner." Jesus said, "I tell you, this man [the tax collector] went down to his house justified rather than the other" (Luke 18:13,14).

That is how we can become righteous. That is how we can get the charges taken from our account. Jesus has already paid the charges. He is waiting for us to bring them to Him to have them cleared from our account. He will clear our record if we will believe that He has paid the price for us. If we will ask Him to be merciful and forgive us, He will do it. That is why He came. He takes our old sin accounts and imputes His righteousness to them. Then we have new accounts. To believe means we become new.

The new person in Christ who has become righteous will then be free to move on to maturity. He can move on to becoming the loving person he wanted to be. As he reads the Word of God, he will see areas in his life that need to be changed and renewed. From that point on he can be moving in the direction of maturing into a new and changed person.

One elderly man I knew was a kind, loving, tenderhearted person. He was understanding, patient, gentle, and meek. He was easy to get along with, and pleasant to work with. He was an encouragement to be around. The sight of his approaching presence always gave me a warm feeling inside. There was a glowing welcome on his face, and I always enjoyed being with him.

Another older man I know is very different. He is set in his ways and in deep ruts. He has a mind and a will of his own which makes him short on patience and love. It is hard to reason with him since he is unable to see the other person's point of view. Accepting and welcoming others are not virtues of his personality. His presence is not welcomed with joy. He keeps me rather uneasy and on edge.

What is the difference in these two people?

Simple! One was experiencing a growing faith in Christ. He was always reaching for more maturity. He was walking above the old ruts of life on a daily walk with Jesus. He stayed prayed-up and tuned-in with God. He experienced a living relationship with God through his Son, Jesus. He didn't remain the same old person, but grew older, wiser, sweeter, and kinder. He was a maturing believer. To believe and walk with Christ means becoming more like Him.

To be a believer, a committed Christian, means we can continually move on toward maturity into a Christlike person. We'll be able to grow in love, kindness, meekness, and tender-heartedness. With God's power we'll be able to change and develop toward being the persons we really want to be.

There is more good news for the person who becomes "new in Christ." He has started a changing process. It is a process that continually changes him toward the mark for which he is reaching. The apostle Paul said, "I press toward the mark for the prize of the high calling of God in Christ Jesus" (Phil. 3:14). It could mean that he had changed toward the mark for the prize.

The person who starts the changing process in this life will experience a climax of change. The Bible explains this change: "Behold, I shew you a mystery; We shall not all sleep, but we shall all be changed, in a moment, in the twinkling of an eye, at the last trump: for the trumpet shall sound, and the dead shall be raised incorruptible, and we shall be changed" (1 Cor. 15:51,52).

Just think! In becoming believers we change from corruptible to incorruptible. The Bible gives more words on the believers' change: "But we all, with open face beholding as in a glass the glory of the Lord, are changed into the same image from glory to glory, even as by the Spirit of the Lord" (2 Cor. 3:18). Can you imagine it? The people who change in Christ will experience the climax of being changed into the glory of the Lord!

On the other hand, to not become a believer means to miss righteousness, to miss becoming new, to live a life of unrighteousness, and to always be the same person — the same old you.

The person who doesn't change in this life will forever beg and pray to be changed. Hell will be a place of moaning and groaning and twisting in anguish, crying to change. But there will be no chance then to change. The changing power will be gone, and there will be a great gulf fixed between the Changer of life and the person who rejected change in this life. To choose not to believe means to miss being changed into the image of the glory of God.

Is it worth it?

7

Having All
You Need

Becoming a believer gives us a relationship with the God who commanded the birds to bring food to one of His hungry servants. It gives us a relationship with the God who makes the sun rise in the East and set in the West each day.

In becoming a Christian we are in contact with the God who sends the rain on both believers and unbelievers. We have a living relationship with the God who "shall supply all your need according to his riches in glory by Christ Jesus" (Phil. 4:19).

Elijah, the prophet, experienced in a dramatic way how God can supply the needs of His people. The prophet had just delivered a message to King Ahab. In this message he told the king there would be no dew or rain for the next several years. Only when Elijah said it would rain would there be moisture.

Then the Lord told Elijah to leave the place quickly. He told Elijah to hide near a brook called Cherith east of Jordan. God promised him food and water at that place.

Elijah must have wondered how he was going to get food in such a place of seclusion, hidden from everyone. However, God met Elijah's need by commanding the ravens to bring him his breakfast and dinner.

God supplied Elijah's need. The Bible tells us that he "went and did according unto the word of the Lord: for he went and dwelt by the brook Cherith, that is before Jordan" (1 Kings 17:5). Elijah obeyed God's instructions. And God followed through on His promise.

Elijah drank water from the brook. Then, when morning came, the ravens brought in his breakfast. They didn't just bring in a box of Coco Pebbles or dry toast with coffee; they brought him bread and meat.

Let's imagine how this might have been. One raven brought a piece of bread, and another brought a piece of meat to lay on top of the bread. A third raven may have brought more bread. And there you have what Howard Estep calls

Elijah's sandwiches — ravenburgers!

In the evening at dinner time, at the Lord's command, the ravens returned with Elijah's dinner. We can imagine it was a steak dinner with dinner rolls. At any rate, God commanded His created birds to supply the need of his servant by flying in bread and meat two times a day.

The Lord told Elijah to go to the town of Zarephath and stay there. So Elijah did as the Lord commanded. When he came to the town gate he saw a widow gathering firewood. He asked her for a drink of water. As she was going, he called after her and asked for some bread too. She explained to him that she didn't have any bread. All she had was a handful of flour and a bit of oil in a jar. "I came here to gather firewood to take home to prepare the meal for my son and me," she said, "that we may eat it and then die."

Elijah told the widow not to panic, but to do what she had planned. But first she was to make him a cake and bring it to Elijah. Then she was to prepare the rest for herself and her son. The prophet then told her God's promise: "The bowl will not run out of flour or the jar run out of oil before the day that I, the Lord, send rain" (1 Kings 17:14; TEV).

The widow did as he said and baked Elijah's cake first. There was flour and oil to supply all their needs, just as God had promised.

Elijah believed and obeyed God. God supplied his need so that Elijah could carry on God's work. Elijah certainly could have testified that believing and obeying resulted in having his needs supplied. God even commanded the birds to supply the needs of his child.

Of course that was a long time ago. Does God still supply for His children today? The Scripture says, "And God is able to give you more than you need, so that you will always have all you need for yourselves and more than enough for every good cause." It also says, "He gives generously to the needy; his kindness lasts forever.

"And God, who supplies seed for the sower and bread to eat, will also supply you with all the seed you need and will make it grow and produce a rich harvest from your generosity. He will always make you rich enough to be generous at all times, so that many will thank God for your gifts which they receive from us. For this service you perform not only meets the needs of God's people, but also produces an outpouring of grateful thanks to God" (2 Cor. 9:9-12; TEV).

God supplies the needs of His people so they can carry out His cause. The above Scripture points out that God will receive thanks for gifts received from others. How Elijah must have thanked God for what the widow shared with him. Believers today thank God for supplying their needs when they receive blessings from others.

I have seen God supply needs many times. I recall the time when my first wife was in the hospital in Pittsburgh, Pennsylvania. Her sudden illness was unexpected and resulted in her being in a coma from Sunday until her death the following Friday. I was unprepared for the week's stay in a strange town.

But as I look back, I see how each need was supplied. Close friends stayed with me through the entire ordeal. One friend used his nine-year-old 1953 Ford for our transportation. Earlier it had given him serious starting problems and one day the car stalled on one of Pittsburgh's steep hill streets. That time, as well as other times during the week, the Ford could have failed to start, but it didn't. It started off there and every other time during the week.

This car was a problem before the hospital experience and again afterward. I believe God supplied my transportation needs for that week. Although it may sound like a minor thing, when a loved one is deathly ill, the absence of car failure was certainly a blessing.

I also marvel how God supplied housing. Someone referred us to several ladies in the city who provided food and lodging near the hospital. Looking back, God supplied in time of need.

Some years later, in 1969, our family needed another car. I was involved in placing Christian books in public places, such as the newsstand at Washington National Airport, that needed regular servicing. A station wagon was what we needed for those transportation purposes, and partly for economy reasons I wanted a standard transmission. After much searching in the ads from the *Washington Post*, I was about at the "end of my rope."

One day, however, I spotted a 1965 Ford wagon in the ads with a standard shift and overdrive. The price was reasonable, and our needs were supplied with an overdrive for a bonus. Almost ten years later, with one engine switch, the car is still serving us well. I believe God supplied this need within a price range we could afford.

Another interesting thing happened when two of us from the Choice Books office were servicing bookracks near Fredericksburg, Virginia. We had taken our inventory on the first rack. Since it was a cold fall day we wanted to start the van and use the heater. The van was dead. When we tried to start it, it sounded like the timing chain had slipped. We thought we were stranded and would probably have to pay to get our van repaired there or have it towed back to our fix-it-yourself home garage.

We went ahead and finished servicing that account, and then we tried to start it again. It started! And it ran the rest of the day while we finished servicing all our stores and it returned us home late that night.

The next morning the van wouldn't start

and we had to replace the timing chain. We believe the timing chain had slipped the day before. God supplied our need and He fixed our van for the day. We were permitted to finish our servicing job and get the van home for repairs.

Now God is not a magic fix-it-all who makes repairs anytime we ask. However, He does know our needs in carrying out His purpose. I couldn't ask God for nine thousand dollars for a new car to use selfishly. But I could expect God to supply our transportation needs.

These incidents are not world-shaking events. They are confirmations along the way in my own personal life that God has the resources to supply the needs of His children in carrying out His purpose. It confirms that we have a personal God who cares for His people in a personal way.

A close friend of ours experienced God's tender supplying care during a crisis experience. This elderly couple from our church was on a vacation visiting their relatives. As they were driving through Minnesota the husband was stricken with a fatal heart attack behind the wheel. His wife didn't drive and wasn't experienced in handling a car. But the car eased off the side of the road into a field and stopped. There was our friend, an elderly woman, in a strange place with her husband dead behind the steering wheel. But when she looked up she saw a man standing by the road, and he had apparently already called for help.

She told us how a policeman then cared for her, took her to his home, and called her family back in Virginia. This policeman and his wife saw that her needs were met until she could be reunited with members of her family. God was there with her to provide for His believer in her time of need.

God also works through a congregation to meet the needs of His people. At our church we established a Brotherly Sharing Fund. This special fund is set up to care for the needs of the congregation. If a member needs to be hospitalized and is faced with the high cost of medical and hospital care, the congregation stands with that member in financial support.

I like this method of meeting the needs of one another. The hospital and medical needs are being met without the high cost of insurance. In time of need the congregation experiences the blessing and unity of sharing with one another. To be a part of God's kingdom and a part of the body of Christ, working together in meeting one another's needs, is indeed a privilege and a blessing.

God is a great provider. The Psalmist says of Him, "For every beast of the forest is mine, and the cattle upon a thousand hills" (Ps. 50:10). God created and owns all the resources in the world. He has ways of providing for His children in need.

In the Sermon on the Mount, Jesus addressed the problems of food and clothing. He taught His followers not to be overanxious about what they would eat, what they would drink, or what they would wear. He taught that they should first seek the kingdom of God: "But seek ye first the kingdom of God, and his righteousness; and all these things shall be added unto you" (Matt. 6:33).

That is a great privilege. When one seeks first the kingdom of God and is a believer, he has the opportunity to be a partner with the great Provider, God himself. God personally has an interest in adding these things "unto you."

To be a believer means you are in touch with the God who "shall supply all your need according to his riches in glory by Christ Jesus." To not be a Christian, to not believe, means you do not draw on the riches in glory to fulfill your needs.

Is it worth it?

8

A Reason for Living

When my son was eight years old, he used to come to me and say, "There's nothing for me to do. What can I do?" Like most of us, he enjoys having something to do. We all want something to do that is of value. Important tasks bring fulfillment into our lives. What is more boring than a whole life with nothing to do? Life without a purpose, without God, or without a mission to fulfill is mere existence.

God has a big plan in mind for the world and mankind. We might say He has a big blueprint that is taking thousands of years to materialize. It started at creation, in the beginning when

God created the heavens and the earth. It continued as God called forth the light and made the day. As He made the firmament, as He gathered together the dry land and called it earth, as He made the green grass, the sun, moon, and stars, and as He created fish, animals, and finally man and woman, His plan continued.

At creation God started a plan for man. This plan will continue through time until God brings in His new heaven and new earth. John saw a vision of this and described it this way:

"And I saw a new heaven and a new earth: for the first heaven and the first earth were passed away; and there was no more sea. And I John saw the holy city, new Jerusalem, coming down from God out of heaven, prepared as a bride adorned for her husband. And I heard a great voice out of heaven saying, Behold, the tabernacle of God is with men, and he will dwell with them, and they shall be his people, and God himself shall be with them, and be their God" (Rev. 21:1-3).

From creation through the years of history until the new heaven comes, God has a big plan in mind. Between creation and the new heaven He calls Christians into this plan to carry it out.

There could be no greater privilege or honor than to serve a King who will be King over all kings. He will be victor over all nations. He will be the King eternal and will reign over all heaven and earth. He is the one to whom every knee will bow and every tongue will confess that He, Jesus, is Lord. The Christian is privileged to fill a slot in the great plan for this King. The Christian is called into building this kingdom here and now. This ministry gives a purpose in life.

Consider the people who have served in God's plan from creation to this present time. Enoch walked with God. Noah built the ark and preserved mankind. Abraham became the father of many nations and received the promise of the Messiah. Through faith, Sarah brought Isaac into the world to carry on the faith. Isaac pronounced blessings on Jacob and Esau, his two sons. Jacob carried on the cause during his time.

Joseph was used to save God's chosen people from famine. Moses was called to deliver the people of God from Egypt's pharaoh. Joshua was used to conquer Jericho. David saved the Israelites from the great giant Goliath and later became king. Esther took the risk of death to save her people.

Isaiah, Jeremiah, Ezekiel, Daniel, Hosea, and others carried on the prophetic message.

Then God called on Mary to bring us Jesus, the Saviour of the world. Jesus himself walked on our earth and called His disciples to carry the good news on to others. John, Peter, Matthew, Mark, Luke, and others fulfilled their purpose by handing the message of the King of kings to their generation of people. Paul found his calling and God made him into an outstanding missionary.

Jesus gave a mission to His followers that is still blessing and changing people's hearts in our world today. After Peter explained the purpose of Christ's coming in his first great sermon, thousands of others believed and joined the cause. Since that time until now, God has given those who respond to Him a ministry to fulfill.

This ministry has led Christians around the world to carry on the cause of Jesus. In spite of all the efforts of earthly kings and nations to destroy the cause and bring it to end, it is still thriving. It has survived the onslaught of persecutions down through the centuries, and it continues to provide people with a purpose for living. God's kingdom does not refuse purposeful living to anyone on grounds of race, nationality, or color. Whoever in the entire world comes to Him in faith will receive a mission for God's kingdom.

In the Old Testament we read of God's instructing Moses to build the tabernacle of the congregation, the ark of the testimony, the mercy seat, and the furniture of the tabernacle. The Lord had a specific job for Moses. Then he spoke to Moses saying, "See, I have called by name Bezaleel . . . and I have filled him with the Spirit of God, in wisdom, and in understanding, and in knowledge, and in all manner of workmanship, to devise cunning works, to work in gold, and in silver, and in brass, and in cutting of stones, to set them, and in carving of timber, to work in all manner of workmanship" (Exod. 31:1-5).

God had a job to be done. He gave Bezaleel the gift and ability to do it. God also gave him a helper named Aholiab. God had a task to be done. He called a man to do it and gave him the wisdom he needed, and He gave him helpers to carry on his work.

God is doing that today. He gives Christians today fulfilling jobs to do. He calls people to declare God's truth and give hope to the hopeless. He calls people to communicate knowledge of God and to make the will of God simple to understand. He calls His people to a new world order of love, where people love others and show that love by deeds of kindness.

God calls people to share their lives with others in giving encouragement and assistance to one another. He asks people to give comfort and compassion to the distressed and lonely. He tells His people to bring a message of good news to the people around the world. God calls His people to a task and He provides the strength for them to carry it out. That strength comes from the presence of God's Holy Spirit.

God is calling leaders to direct the people of God through today's world. He calls some to be teachers, some to be pastors, and some to be evangelists. Paul wrote, "God set the members every one of them in the body, as it hath pleased him" (1 Cor. 12:18). God has a place in His program for everyone. He has a purpose for every person to fulfill.

Jesus gives each a mission and a purpose for living. God has delivered us from the "power of darkness, and hath translated us into the kingdom of his dear Son" (Col. 1:12-14). Think of it, if you become a Christian you can be delivered from the power of darkness and be transferred to a position in Christ's kingdom! That is what happened to Peter, the man who denied Christ. He repented and he was transferred into the kingdom of Jesus. He was then given a ministry that is influencing the world yet today.

The Bible tells us that our Lord has "called us with an holy calling, not according to our works, but according to his own purpose and grace, which was given us in Christ Jesus before the world began" (2 Tim. 1:9). What a privilege it is to be called with a holy calling before the world even began.

Jesus said, "A good man out of the good treasure of the heart bringeth forth good things" (Matt. 12:35). When a person finds his mission in Christ's kingdom, he brings forth good things. He is transferred from a nobody to a somebody. Christ transforms people — He makes alcoholics into ministers, helpers from beggars, and honorable individuals from murderers.

Contrast evil, hatred, destruction, sorrow, grief, and disappointments with the mission Christ gives. An illustration of this contrast is the confession of R.E. Walton in *The Language of the Death Bed* by D. J. Stutzman:

> My companions were the very lowest. For at the age of fifteen years I started to mingle with the degraded men and women, who taught me to do everything they could think of that was bad, until I fell so low I was hardly able to get up again. Then I became a thief and was sent to prison five times, where I passed the best part of my life, until today I find myself facing death by the hangman's rope to pay the penalty for one of my crimes. But the way of the transgressor of the law is hard, and after I am sleeping that long sleep that knows no waking I want every man and woman, boy and girl, in this large city of Chicago to come and take a last look at me and then go away thinking and thinking deeply; for in looking upon my face they will have a chance to see what a life of crime and sin will do for you.

On the other hand, Paul is an example of Christ's transformations of people. He said, "The time of my departure is at hand. I have fought a good fight, I have finished my course, I have kept the faith" (2 Tim. 4:6,7). Paul accomplished a mission. He made a contribution to his generation and to all people after him. Therefore, he could say, "Henceforth there is laid up for me a crown of righteousness, which the Lord, the righteous judge, shall give me at that day" (2 Tim. 4:8).

Paul further said that this crown was not just for him, "but unto all them also that love his appearing" (2 Tim. 4:8). In 1 Thessalonians 2:12 He wrote that God hath "called you unto his kingdom and glory." That is what Paul experienced in his own life: a purpose, a ministry, a mission, a reason for living. Because he was in Christ, he could take inventory of himself and say, "I have fought a good fight."

It can be just the same for Christians. God has a mission for every believer. Each believer is called according to God's purpose and is given a worthy mission. According to Jesus, giving a cup of cold water in his name is a worthy cause in His kingdom. "For whosoever shall give you a cup of water to drink in my name, because ye belong to Christ, verily I say unto you, he shall not lose his reward" (Mark 9:41).

In the kingdom of God we count. We are more than an unknown name on a tombstone or a long number on a computer card. Our names are written in the Book of Life which the Bible talks about in Philippians 4:3 and in Revelation

20:15. The Book of Life is a register of all names that belong in God's kingdom. Having our name registered there and being part of the Kingdom that lasts forever is the greatest treasure any person can have.

In contrast to the Christians, those who choose not to belong to the kingdom of Christ will not be rewarded for any of the great things they have done. Jesus said of them, "Many will say to me in that day, Lord, Lord, have we not prophesied in thy name? and in thy name have cast out devils? and in thy name done many wonderful works? And then will I profess unto them, I never knew you: depart from me, ye that work iniquity" (Matt. 7:22,23). To miss the kingdom of God means to miss our reward. The kind or size of great deeds that we do is not what counts, but to whom we belong is the important thing. If we don't belong to Jesus, we miss out on His rewards.

To miss the kingdom of Christ and the purpose He has for us is really missing life. Is anything worse than a life with nothing valuable accomplished? T. Cecil Meyers reports in *Living on Tiptoe* that "each year twenty thousand people take their lives, and every four minutes someone tries." He states further, "Psychologists report that one of the major reasons is that whereas we have plenty to live on, far too many of us have nothing to live for, no sense of purpose, no far-reaching hope, that makes life infinitely worthwhile.

And there it is. To not be a Christian means we would miss our purpose of being. Like my son, we would have "nothing to do."

Is it worth it?

9

Protection for You

In 1959 I took a job at the Children's Hospital in Washington, DC. I worked evenings and shortly before twelve the midnight shift came on duty and I was relieved. One evening, with my day's work behind me, I headed my 1950 Ford out of the city for the country. I had a four-hour drive ahead of me.

The drive was relaxing as I breezed through the countryside with car lights now and then shining their rays at me. The stillness of the after-midnight hours had soon relaxed me too much, and sleepiness came over me. I realized I had dozed behind the wheel when I was suddenly awakened by a loud sharp bang. In front of me was a sharp curve. The Ford cornered the curve all right and continued west on Route 7 toward Winchester, Virginia.

What was the bang just before the curve? Was it God? Was it a guardian angel? I knew it had to have come from God. Maybe He sent an angel in answer to someone's prayer for me. I don't know what God used to cause the noise, but I believe He awakened me from sleep in time to make that curve safely.

This experience reminded me that God wasn't finished with me yet. He had something more for me to do in working out His own good purposes. He protected His cause and plan for me.

Jesus said to His disciples, "I am with you always, even unto the end of the world" (Matt. 28:20). His care is present with all believers to protect His cause. God's protection was demonstrated on the island of Malta to His servant Paul, who was at that time a prisoner. It was determined that Paul should be transported to Italy with some other prisoners who were turned over to an officer named Julius.

The group set sail on the Mediterranean about mid-September. The weather this time of year made sailing dangerous. As they were sailing, a soft south wind began to blow. A little later the wind grew stronger, and as the wind hit the ship it became impossible to keep the ship headed into the wind. So the captains gave up and allowed the ship to be carried along with the wind.

As the violent storm continued, the passengers threw some of the cargo and equipment overboard to increase their chance of survival. After the men had gone a long time without food, Paul stood before them and told them of God's protection. "But now I beg you, take courage! Not one of you will lose his life; only the ship will be lost. For last night an angel of the God to whom I belong and whom I worship came to me and said, 'Don't be afraid, Paul! You must stand before the Emperor. And God, in his goodness to you, has spared the lives of all those who are sailing with you.' So take courage, men! For I trust in God that it will be just as I was told. But we will be driven ashore on some island" (Acts 27:22-26; TEV).

The persons on the ship experienced fourteen nights of storm, and at times the outlook seemed hopeless. Then one day the ship "hit a sandbank and went aground; the front part of the ship got stuck and could not move, while the back part was being broken to pieces by the violence of the waves."

The soldiers planned then to kill all the prisoners to keep them from swimming ashore and escaping. But since the army officer wanted to save Paul, he didn't allow the soldiers to carry out the plan. Instead, he ordered those who could swim to jump overboard, and the rest were to follow by grabbing onto planks and pieces of the ship. Everyone arrived safely ashore on the island of Malta.

It was cold and raining when they landed. The natives on the island built a warming fire to welcome them. Paul helped gather sticks and was putting them on the fire when a snake came out of the woods and fastened itself on Paul's hand. The natives saw the snake and consequently decided Paul was a murderer. Paul shook the snake off into the fire and the people expectantly watched for his hand to swell up and for him to fall over dead. After waiting a long time and seeing that nothing happened to him, they decided instead he was a god.

At sea and on the island, God protected Paul, His believer. His special protection was upon him. He protected him from the storm, the violent water, the shipwreck, and the snakebite. God protects His people to carry on His cause.

The account of Daniel is recorded in the Old Testament. Because of Daniel's trust in God he was in the habit of praying three times each day to Him. Some of Daniel's colleagues were jealous of Daniel's high position. Through a conspiracy they had a law put into effect that stated if any man prayed to any god or man other than King Darius for the coming thirty days, he would be cast into a den of lions.

Still Daniel believed in the God of heaven. He continued his prayer relationship as he was accustomed to doing. He knew the risk of the lions' den, but he believed in God.

When King Darius realized the consequences and motive of the law he had given his approval to, he was sorry that he had allowed himself to be tricked into such a law. However, the law was made and it could not be changed. Daniel was cast into a den of fierce and hungry lions.

God was not finished with Daniel and it was in His good purpose to protect him. As Daniel came scooting into the lions' den, the hungry lions got angelic lockjaw. Their mouths were shut by a power greater than the lions themselves.

Daniel described it like this in a reply to the King: "My God hath sent his angel, and hath shut the lions' mouths, that they have not hurt me" (Dan. 6:22). When Daniel was taken up out of the den, no injury was found on him. Daniel was a believer. God protected Daniel for His cause and Daniel knew God's protection.

David, in one of his psalms, says of God, "You . . . protect those who love you; because of you they are truly happy. You bless those who obey you, Lord; your love protects them like a shield" (Ps. 5:11,12; TEV). David could have written these words from his own life experiences and from what he observed in others.

The Book of Acts tells how Peter was miraculously delivered and protected from a violent king. King Herod saw that it pleased the Jews when he had James, the brother of John, killed by the sword. Therefore, since the public mood was in his favor (the polls would have supported him), he proceeded in his plans to have Peter killed, too. Peter was apprehended and put into prison where he was guarded by four squads of soldiers, with four soldiers in each squad.

Together, the believers earnestly prayed for Peter the night before he was to be taken out of prison and brought before the public. Peter, meanwhile, was sleeping between two of the guards. He was securely tied with chains, and more guards were on duty to watch the gates.

The believing Church was in prayer when God sent an angel to awaken Peter. God's power caused the chains to fall off Peter's hands. The angel commanded Peter to follow him out of the prison. They passed both guard stations, and the iron gate opened up for them to walk through. "Then Peter realized what had happened to him and he said, 'Now I know that it is really true! The Lord sent his angel to rescue me from Herod's power and from everything the Jewish people expected to happen' " (Acts 12:11; TEV).

Peter, the believer, was protected for God's own good cause. When you believe, you can be assured that God will protect His own cause in you. It is no wonder that Peter could write in his epistle, "Casting all your anxiety upon Him, because He cares for you" (1 Pet. 5:7; NAS). In this passage, believers are invited to cast all their cares, worries, and anxieties upon God. God is waiting to hear them. He is waiting to give grace and deliverance.

Believers constantly seek God's protecting hand as they pass through this life. The Bible says, "He is a shield unto them that put their trust in him" (Prov. 30:5).

Believers have the promise of protection from God's wrath. When God judges the world, when He pours out His wrath on the unrighteous, the righteous will be protected. As the Bible says, "Much more then, being now justified by his blood, we shall be saved from wrath through him" (Rom. 5:9).

Believers have a God to call upon for protection now. We also have the promise of protection from His wrath in the future. Nonbelievers, on the other hand, are outside God's divine purpose and protection; they are outside the deliverance from the wrath of God. Missing God's protection and deliverance is a big price to pay for not being a believer.

Is it worth it?

10

Be on the Winning Side

In any political campaign there is a victor and a loser. While one side holds a victory party, the opponent is expected to come forth with a statement conceding loss. The person who experiences life in Christ is on the victory side. He will be part of the final victory celebration.

Near Richmond, Virginia, there is an elegant restaurant offering a noon buffet at a reasonable price. When my business partner and I stopped in to try it out, we were met at the door by a waitress who ushered us to our table. After we were instructed to help ourselves, we were led to a place where there was plenty of good food laid out in a tasteful atmosphere. We could help ourselves to all we wanted. "This way, please" led us to a feast.

The Holy Spirit is the waitress of the Church. The Holy Spirit stands at the heart's door and invites the believer to come "right this way" into victory. When the believer enters that dining hall of victory he is filled with victory and freedom. Victory belongs to him because God gave him the gift of the Holy Spirit.

Life is a battleground and a testing period. It is the time when one decides if he will be defeated or if he will celebrate with the victory party.

Victory Over Sin

To a person who places his faith in Christ and commits his life for His cause, God gives a strength greater than himself. God baptizes the believer with the Holy Spirit into the body of Christ. God's Spirit indwells the believer and waits to usher the believer into victory and freedom. Like a good host, He is ready to lead us into a "freedom room" where we can enjoy victory over sin. Jesus came to forgive sin and release the believer from its grip. Jesus told the woman who stood weeping behind Him, washing His feet with her tears, "Thy sins are forgiven . . . Thy faith hath saved thee; go in peace" (Luke 7:48,50).

Jesus, the Lord, spoke words of victory to the thief who hung on a cross dying beside Him: "Today shalt thou be with me in paradise" (Luke 23:43).

The Bible gives these hopeful words to the believer when his armor is down and he commits sin: "If any man sin, we have an advocate with the Father, Jesus Christ, the righteous" (1 John 2:1). God is willing to restore our fellowship with Him if we come in repentance and confession, and if we believe.

There is more good news from the Bible on freedom from sin: "There hath no temptation taken you but such as is common to man: but God is faithful, who will not suffer you to be tempted above that ye are able; but will with the temptation also make a way to escape, that ye may be able to bear it" (1 Cor. 10:13).

The first piece of good news is that we do not have any unusual temptations. We aren't the only ones with our problem. It could be that some of our best friends are being tested and tried in some of the same areas we are. Sharing our trial area and seeking help are ways in which the Spirit leads us into victory.

The second bit of good news is that God will not allow us to be tempted above what we can handle. Our temptations are pretested, they are checked out against us to see if we can take them. Our temptations are really tests that can strengthen us. As the Bible says, "Count it all joy when ye fall into divers temptations; knowing this, that the trying of your faith worketh patience" (James 1:2,3).

Patience and endurance are qualities everyone needs. They are developed in our life by passing the tests and being victorious over temptation. What actually seems to be our enemy can become our friend. Temptations turned into victory produce strength and growth. It means moving into freedom from sin and growing in victorious living.

The third piece of good news is that there is a "way of escape." God provides an exit door. The way to victory is already provided. When we are under temptation or when the load gets heavy, we can take it to God. We can tell Him our struggle and let Him hear us acknowledge that it is too much for us to bear alone. When we honestly seek His strength, the Holy Spirit provides a way through by empowering us to go through the escape exit. At the darkest hour God will let the dawn break through and the victory light will shine. For the believer, there is victory provided over sin. That is good news!

Victory Over Self

The Holy Spirit is also ready to lead the believer into victory over self-centeredness. To live on the victory side we need to be free from ourselves. We need to experience freedom from our selfish desires and our selfish past.

Take the person who has made a decision and followed through with it, and it turns out all wrong. Rather than accepting the failure and breaking free through repentance and confession to move on with life, he spends the rest of his life trying to prove he was right. His own self-conceit prevents him from experiencing release and victory over the past and exploring new adventures in living here now.

Or consider the person who permitted himself to react negatively to a church problem. He got fed up and left the church. Later indications showed that he made the wrong move. Instead of owning his failure and breaking free, he defends the wrong decision for the rest of his life. He wastes his precious time running down the church and tries to justify his own mistakes.

The Holy Spirit wants to lead such persons into victory experiences to free them from themselves. The Spirit provides power to become free and to live in victory over ourselves. As we acknowledge our past failures to God, His Spirit will empower us to make amends with our fellow associates and live a fulfilled life in the kingdom of God.

I believe the apostle Paul had a taste of this freedom from self when he wrote, "I press toward the mark for the prize of the high calling of God in Christ Jesus" (Phil. 3:14). The Christian can live on the victory side and be free from the selfishness that seeks wealth for himself. He can possess a kind of love that "seeketh not her own" (1 Cor. 13:5).

I know a man who carried a grudge and a burden against another man for years. He became deadlocked in his feelings and simply couldn't escape the feelings of disappointment, revenge, and anger he had over the way he had once been treated. Well-meaning friends told him to just "forgive and forget." However, the hurt was so deeply inflicted that forgetting was impossible. He became like an outcast and a vagabond. Ulcers were eating away at his stomach and his health began to slip away. The doctor wanted to do heart surgery. His spirit and his physical health had almost hit bottom.

Then one night this man opened up to me and told his side of the story. As he talked he vented his frustrations. The night wore on and we talked of the forgiving and forgetting that his friends had advised him to do. It wasn't that simple for him and that was understandable. The hurt had been deeply inflicted. Every time he saw the person who hurt him, he ached in the pit of his stomach. How was it possible for him to forgive and be free from his own bitterness?

Finally, late that night, forgiveness began to make sense. It doesn't mean to just forget. It means to drop all charges against the other. It means to cancel all the angry demands of restitution required from the other person.

Certainly with each time one sees the person who has offended him there is a hurt feeling. But he can forgive each time. As he feels the demands come up the spine of his back, he drops them again. He cancels his demands. He lets the offender go free.

Suppose he sees that person 490 times in one day and he feels the hurt 490 times? Forgive — 490 times! That is what Jesus asked His followers to do in Matthew 18:22. Forget it? Not necessarily. Hurts and pains cannot soon be forgotten. However, they can be forgiven.

As the night wore on and dawn began to break over the mountains, forgiveness began to be possible for my friend. By noon he willed to forgive, and in doing so he took a giant step to free himself. In the best way he knew, he dropped the charges and canceled the demands he had made. Healing began to happen at that moment.

In the weeks, months, and years that followed, the hurt continued to heal. So did the ulcers and the heart problem. The heart surgery hasn't been considered recently. Spiritual growth came and matured. This man is living again. God's Spirit led him to victory. What a blessing to be a believer!

Victory over the System

Jesus also gives victory over the system

which the Bible calls "the world." The world system has put a tremendous pressure on believers. The call to conform to its standards comes from all angles. This passing world wants our attention, our loyalty, our allegiance, and our money. We are constantly being pressured to keep up with the system, to change and to conform to its jet age image.

Since the world system has not found satisfaction and fulfillment, it keeps seeking more ways to gratify its desires. The system is constantly changing. It is thinking up new ways to stir up discontentment with the things we now own. It is trying to make us unhappy with what we have so we'll spend more. We are invited to charge it, try it for thirty days, or call for a free demonstration. Things like these hook us to put our money into the system.

The pressures are upon us to conform and get in the struggle for wealth and accumulate temporal things. Pressures from the social world, the business world, the community, newspapers, magazines, television, and mail invite us to shape into the world's standards. Trying to keep up in the rat race is tiring, exhausting, frustrating, nerve-racking, heart-attacking, and ulcerating.

By becoming a Christians we can break free from this mess. The Holy Spirit is ready to usher us into victory over the system. The *Good News Bible* says, "Do not conform yourselves to the standards of this world" (Rom. 12:2; TEV). When we conform to this world, our mind is set on things of the present life and the pleasures we can attain here now. A worldly person seeks fulfillment of life in this world and with what it can offer.

Jesus came to such a world to give deliverance and victory. He said of His followers, "They are not of the world, even as I am not of the world" (John 17:16). His prayer was not to have them taken out of the world, but that they should be kept from the evil of it.

He stands ready to set us free from silly styles, drugs, alcohol, tobacco, filth, sex perversion, hatred, malice, strife, and any other evils that downgrade us. Jesus was concerned that His followers experience freedom and victory over this world. He wants us to be free and unattached to this world so we can have complete freedom to carry on His work until He comes again. He wants His followers to be free to carry on the work of His kingdom.

What is worldly? I believe anything that detracts us from allegiance and commitment to God is worldly and of this world system. Anything that draws away from service, from doing work in the kingdom of God here and now, is of this world. Anything we permit to take our time, energy, and money away from living for God is of this world and is contrary to His interests.

The wicked one is interested in our devotion

and wants our service. The Bible says, "Love not the world, neither the things that are in the world. If any man love the world, the love of the Father is not in him" (1 John 2:15).

The god of this world wants our love. The God of heaven wants our love. We cannot love both. The world system wants us to obey when it gives the signals. On the other hand, God wants us to obey His Word and then live and practice it here and now. There is a deep satisfaction in being God's separated person here in this present world. It is a gratifying experience to be living above the power of the system and to be engrossed in the work of God's kingdom.

The good news is that we believers can experience freedom and victory. We can be cut loose from the mad race of the establishment. We can be different and free and live with the greatest purpose in the world.

We are not strong enough to live above this world of ourselves. However, God gave us His Spirit to live within us. He is greater than the world. He gives victory to those who yield fully to Him. The Bible says, "Greater is he that is in you, than he that is in the world" (1 John 4:4). The one "greater" than the world gives victory and purpose of living. What an exciting and liberating experience!

To believe means we can live victoriously over sin, self, and the system and have a purpose in life that brings rewards forever. We will be part of the victory climax when "death is swallowed up in victory" (1 Cor. 15:54). "To him that overcometh will I give to eat of the tree of life" (Rev. 1:7).

However, to not believe means to settle for second-rate life controlled by the spirit of the world.

Is it worth it?

11

Don't Miss Your Inheritance

Suppose you were a child of a multimillionaire and your father owned a huge mansion on a large tract of land. Your father has willed the whole estate and his money to you. If you don't die before he does, you will receive the inheritance. Being the child of a rich father does not guarantee that we will become wealthy. However, being the child of the heavenly Father does guarantee us an inheritance of wealth.

Some religious followers pile wealth and fame on to their leaders. The followers are often led to believe that their personal discomforts are trials and tribulations that make them strong. They live in poverty and sacrifice their lives collecting funds to increase the leader's wealth. This is often done in the name of helping the poor, aiding youth, and helping drug addicts. At the same time the leaders live in luxury, wasting the money on expensive clothes, the finest cars, and extravagant mansions. These religious leaders simply draw from the wealth of their followers to hoard it for themselves.

In November 1978 a shock went around the world as the news was released of the murder of Congressman Leo Ryan on his investigative trip of Jonestown in Guyana. Jim Jones, the leader of the Jonestown cult, had deceived a group of people into giving him their loyalty and their belongings. He led them to believe in him and to do exactly what he requested. He finally misled them into partaking in the shocking act of mass suicide where over nine hundred people died.

This religious leader stripped his people of their dignity, their character, their belongings, and finally talked them into joining him in a ghastly act of suicide. In the form of religion he deprived his followers of what they had and robbed them of their own lives. The climax of this movement was an appalling tragedy of downright deception.

Christianity is very different from these forms of religion. The leader of Christianity was willing to lay down His life for the lives of His

followers. He was willing to take the consequences of sin upon himself and personally pay
the penalty for it. He went to the grave. But then
He rose again alive! He is now the Living Leader
of Christianity.

Jesus didn't seek and hoard wealth for himself. In fact, He promised the opposite to His
followers. While He was on Earth He left this
promise: "In my Father's house are many
mansions . . . I go to prepare a place for you . . .
I will come again, and receive you unto myself;
that where I am, there ye may be also (John
14:2,3). Look at the promises: There are many
mansions! There is a place prepared for you!
Jesus himself will come to bring you into His
presence! Only Christianity can offer such an
inheritance.

Jesus could promise a mansion prepared for
us because as Christians we are children of God.
We are joint heirs with Christ. Therefore, what
is God's, will be ours. God is rich in mansions
and lands and we are His heirs. "Wherefore thou
art no more a servant, but a son; and if a son,
then an heir of God through Christ" (Gal. 4:7).

The *Good News Bible* states the case this
way: "But now to continue — the son who will
receive his father's property is treated just like
a slave while he is young, even though he really
owns everything. While he is young, there are
men who take care of him and manage his
affairs until the time set by his father. In the

same way, we too were slaves of the ruling spirits of the universe before we reached spiritual maturity. But when the right time finally came, God sent His own Son. He came as the son of a human mother and lived under the Jewish law to redeem those who were under the law, so that we might become God's sons. To show that we are his sons, God sent the Spirit of his Son into our hearts, the Spirit who cries out, 'Father, my Father.' So then, you are no longer a slave but a son. And since you are his son, God will give you all that he has for his sons" (Gal. 4:1-8;TEV).

Think of it. To become a believer is to become a son. And becoming a son is becoming a joint heir with God through Christ. Christianity promises an inheritance to us. No other religion can offer and deliver such an eternal inheritance.

Christianity not only gives an eternal inheritance, it also provides the services of an attorney to settle the Christian's case. Jesus is the Christian's attorney and He will plead the case of the Christian to the Heavenly Father. To be a believer means to have attorney Jesus handling our case so that we inherit the Kingdom and live in the mansions built especially for us. Jesus himself said, "Whosoever therefore shall confess me before men, him will I confess also before my Father which is in heaven" (Matt. 10:32).

From these words of Jesus we have the promise that if we confess Him in this present life, He will represent us to the Heavenly Father. Jesus becomes our personal attorney who pleads our case to the Father, the righteous Judge. He knows each of us, and Jesus will say, "This is my child. He is a believer who shall inherit the kingdom." Then the Judge will say, "Enter thou into the joy of my Lord."

What a thrill to know that being a Christian means having a personal attorney to represent my case to the Judge! No other religion can make such a promise.

Satan, the devil, is an accuser of the Christians. He tells us we are guilty and accuses them of being sinners. He will send his opposing forces to convince you that you are guilty before God. He is right on that one account.

Our life is like a huge file cabinet. All the deeds we have done are recorded and filed away. In the drawers are files that record all our sins. Sin after sin is filed away, waiting to be pulled out against us on the judgment day. Satan will try to tell us that there is no use believing because our sins are on record. He tells us that we are guilty, that we need to be condemned and sent to everlasting punishment. Satan is right on that, but he has already lost the believer's case.

When we confess our sinfulness to Jesus and asks for forgiveness, we receive forgiveness. Our sins are covered by the shed blood of Jesus Christ. Therefore, the Judge cannot see them anymore. The Bible says, "The accuser of our brethren is cast down, which accused them before our God day and night. And they overcame him by the blood of the Lamb" (Rev. 12:10,11).

Suppose you were in a courtroom and were guilty of a crime. The judge hears your case and looks at your attorney asking if you are guilty. The attorney simply says yes, but he himself will pay all the fines so you can go free. That is what the Christian's attorney has already done. People become Christians by believing and trusting in the sacrifice that Jesus already paid. He paid the price with His own blood so that now Christians can go free.

Christians are not perfect people. We are the ones who realize we transgress God's law and are sinful by nature. We are the ones who have taken our transgression case to attorney Jesus and asked forgiveness and pardon. We are the ones whom Jesus has forgiven and set free from the guilt and penalty of sin. Jesus will handle our case. He will "say unto them on his right hand, Come ye blessed of my Father, inherit the kingdom prepared for you from the foundation of the world" (Matt. 25:34).

To be a Christian and have life means we have someone handling our case for us. It means we will receive an inheritance.

On the other hand, to not be a Christian is like the son of a wealthy deceased father who has no attorney to take his case and consequently loses the wealth and the estate. To not be a Christian means we have no one to plead our case. It means we miss being an heir, and we miss our inheritance. It's a high price to pay for missing life!

Is it worth it?

12

Enjoy God's Presence

In this present life when we receive an inheritance, it means that our father or ancestor has died. As heirs or heiresses we cannot enjoy the wealthy inheritance and the presence of the ancestor at the same time.

However, for Christians, it is different. We receive an inheritance and we are privileged to enjoy the actual presence of God at the same time. Their Lord and Saviour has died; therefore the believers can receive their inheritance. But the difference is that the the Lord didn't stay dead in the grave. He died and made settlement of provisions with God the Father for the sins of everyone. Then He arose alive.

The grave, the stone in front of the opening, the government with its armed guards, and all the forces of Satan couldn't keep Christ in the grave. He arose and is alive and He will be alive forever. The living Saviour himself burst out of the grave and is alive and He will be alive forever.

And better yet, Christ himself will be with each of us. The believer has the living presence of the Saviour when he receives his inheritance. He will then be "safe in the arms of Jesus" as a songwriter once wrote. The person who has established a relationship with God here in this life will have a continuing and extended relationship beyond this life. The Bible calls it eternal life. It is a forever relationship.

Imagine strolling through a park on a beautiful warm afternoon. Looking across the park you see a young boy and girl sitting on one of the benches. They are looking face to face at one another and talking seriously. They are deeply interested in each other. You may be witnessing the beginning of a relationship in which the two walk together, talk together, and eventually enter into marriage.

This scene illustrates the meaning of a relationship with God. Like the young couple who excitingly start a dating relationship, so the believer establishes a relationship with God. He and God talk together, walk together, drive together, work together, and live together. God's presence is in the believer through the Holy Spirit.

When we enjoy this kind of relationship with God we will be conforming to God's will. Our life will be shaped by God's love letter, the Bible.

Does this beautiful relationship cease when life ceases? No! For the ones who have discovered life with God here, the relationship will continue. That relationship will put us into the very presence of God in a new heaven and a holy city.

Just think of it! To be believers means we have eternal life and a relationship with God. We will be living in the presence of God himself. The Bible describes it like this: "Behold, the tabernacle of God is with men, and he will dwell with them, and they shall be his people, and God himself shall be with them, and be their God" (Rev. 21:3).

This relationship with God is a forever relationship, it will never end. "So shall we ever be with the Lord" (1 Thess. 4:17).

One Sunday a man came to my door peddling his religion. He talked about future events and about Jehovah. After some discussion and questions I discovered that the best he expects for himself is to live with Christ for a thousand years. Then for him it would all be over. That is not the kind of relationship the believer has in Christ. His relationship will be "forever with the Lord."

In this forever relationship, God's personal touch will be there. The Bible tells us that "God shall wipe away all tears from their eyes; and there shall be no more death, neither sorrow, nor crying, neither shall there be any more pain: for the former things are passed away" (Rev. 21:4). Rescue squads, doctors, hospitals, and funeral coaches are things of the past when our relationship with God continues.

God becomes the light of the city and stamps out darkness forever in that new world. As the Bible says, "There shall be no night there; and they need no candle, neither light of the sun; for the Lord God giveth them light: and they shall reign for ever and ever" (Rev. 22:5).

The glory of God will lighten the city. There will be no fuel shortages there, no blackouts, and no inflated energy bills. God's glory will provide light forever and ever.

Imagine walking on streets of gold. There will be no more potholes and bad roads because of lack of funds in heaven. "The street of the city was pure gold" (Rev. 21:21).

Imagine coming to the "marriage supper of the Lamb." Imagine the tree of life that bears fruit every month. Imagine the "water of life," a river clear as crystal, pouring out of the throne of God. Just imagine — fruit that hasn't been sprayed and water that hasn't been contaminated!

Imagine joining in the singing of a new song and being part of the great number singing the song of Moses and the Lamb. Imagine being a part of the greatest choir that ever was, singing praises face to face with Jesus. "And they shall see his face" (Rev. 22:4).

Can you imagine a city with no taxes? No more hunger and thirst? No more hospitals or graves? There will be no partings! All of those will be gone, and there will be so much more in the very presence of God as the believer's relationship with Him goes on forever and ever.

Marshall Pak told this story of a young boy who left home to be on his own and to live his own life. Somewhat like the prodigal son, he finally decided to return home. It was twenty years after he left that he walked down "that same old road" toward home.

> The weeds had grown so high I could scarcely see the wagon tracks. As I neared the old home place, my heart skipped a beat. And, neighbors, I think it stopped beating as I opened the rusty old iron gate leading up the walk. The door stood wide open on its weather-beaten hinges. I stood silent for a moment. Then I called aloud in a trembling voice, "Anybody home? Hello there!"

The only answer was the sigh of the wind through the pine trees, and in that moment I knew there would be no one to welcome me home. As I walked amid the memories of my childhood days in those empty rooms, the hot tears of regret poured down my face. Oh, Lord, if I could but turn back the years, if only I could have taken time to write to those I loved. The hot tears almost blinded me as I stumbled through the hallway into the backyard. Like a lost child calling for his mother, I called again and again for mother. But there was no answer, only the sighs of the soft winds.

Those who choose not to be a Christian will have no one to welcome them home. At the end of this life there will be no heavenly persons to welcome them into that beautiful home. They'll miss it all.

On the other hand, for the Christian it is very different. The Bible says, "Yea, though I walk through the valley of the shadow of death, I will fear no evil: for thou art with me" (Ps. 23:4).

When I was a small boy I used to walk across the meadow with my big brother. We would come to a stream we had to cross. It always looked too big for me to jump over. But when my big brother crossed over and reached his big hand back to me I felt secure. His big hand took me safely across.

When the Christian comes to the end of this present life, there will be someone there to welcome him home. Jesus will be there to take him across into the presence of God. And he will dwell and live in the presence of the Lord forever. "And God himself shall be with them, and be their God" (Rev. 21:3). To the believer that means someone will be there.

To choose not to be a Christian means to miss being with the most loving Person who ever walked on Earth, Jesus. Here on this planet Earth we hear of people with whom we "just can't stand to live." The non-Christian will be spending forever with the deceiver, the liar, the devil himself. He will live in eternity with a person he just can't stand. That is a high price to pay for not being a Christian. Missing the presence of Jesus and the heavenly city is costly. Is it worth it?

Being a Christian is a small price to pay to be able to be ushered into the presence of God to live in a prepared mansion with Him forever. That is worth it!

About the Author

From country to city ... tasting sorrow and finding victory . . . a simple life committed to Christ ... and a desire to spread the gospel ... these are all characteristics of Simon Schrock of Fairfax, Virginia.

Born in 1936 in Oakland, Maryland, to Amish parents, Simon became a Christian and a member of the Amish Mennonite Church. During his childhood years, he knew the serenity of life in rural Appalachia, attending a one-room school and a country church.

After his marriage to Eva Lena Yoder, Simon moved to Washington, DC, and felt the contrast of the smoky, noisy city. He began passing out Christian literature as he moved about the city. The death of his young wife led him through some deep soul-searching, but it ultimately deepened his commitment to Christ. Pauline (Polly) Yoder and Simon were married about a year later.

In 1968 Simon was introduced to the Christian bookrack ministry. He began dreaming of providing good literature for travelers passing through the Washington National Airport, and he placed his first inspirational books in the airport during that year. Since 1968, Simon has been instrumental in the sale of over 166,000 books at the two Washington airports.

The Price of Missing Life grows out of Simon's concern to provide wholesome, inspirational reading material to the public. He lives on the cutting edge of his own denomination and participates in evangelistic outreach through preaching, writing, and speaking engagements. It is from this perspective that Simon writes. He is a warmhearted Christian whose life exemplifies what it means to live in obedience to Christ.

Simon believes that life is worth living and that life at its best includes a commitment to the lordship of Jesus Christ. To miss the Christian life, and consequently heaven, is a high price to pay.